Fighting Colors

USAF EUROPE
VOLUME 2
1947-1963

in Color

by Robert Robinson
Illustrated by Robert Robinson

squadron/signal publications

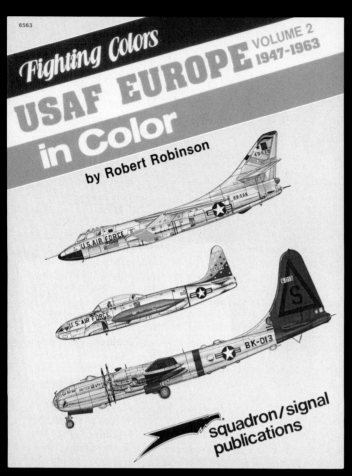

Cover: (Top to Bottom)

A Douglas RB-66B (54-528) assigned to the 30th Tactical Reconnaissance Squadron at Alconbury, Huntingshire, during 1960.

This T-33A (53-5819) was used by the 81st Tactical Fighter Wing Base Flight during 1963.

A Boeing B-50A (46-013) of the 96th Bomb Squadron at Lakenheath Air Base during early 1950.

If you have any photographs of the aircraft, armor, soldiers or ships of any nation, particularly wartime snapshots, why not share them with us and help make Squadron/Signal's books all the more interesting and complete in the future. Any photograph sent to us will be copied and the original returned. The donor will be fully credited for any photos used. Please send them to:

Squadron/Signal Publications, Inc.
1115 Crowley Drive.
Carrollton, TX 75011-5010.

ISBN 0-89747-250-0

ACKNOWLEDGEMENTS

A work of this type cannot be accomplished without the kind help and assistance of a number of people. I would like to thank, in particular, Dave Menard, George Pennick, COL John Harris, Dave Mitchell, James Bruggeman, A. Hague and Headquarters USAF HRC/RI, Maxwell AFB.

A Black bellied B-29 (44-86257) of the 97th Bomb Wing on the ramp at RAF Marham, Norfolk, during one of the training and goodwill flights conducted by the USAF during June of 1947. (MAP)

Introduction

With the end of the Second World War, the U.S. Eighth Air Force began withdrawing its aircraft, equipment and personnel from the well over a hundred British bases from which the 8th had fought the war. The last of these bases, RAF Honington, was vacated during February of 1946.

At the time, only a few in either Britain or America could have foreseen the return of USAF aircraft to British soil after a gap of just three years. Although Europe was at peace, it was a peace filled with tension between the Western Allies and the Soviet Union.

With the formation of the U.S. Air Force as a separate service during 1947, a reorganization of the Air Force command structure took place. One of the newly formed USAF commands was to be based in England under the title, United States Air Forces in Europe (USAFE). Initially, USAFE's primary mission was overseeing the deployment of Air Force strategic and tactical units rotating in and out of bases in Europe.

Strategic Air Command

During the mid to late 1940s USAFE was occupied with supporting the movement of men and aircraft of the Strategic Air Command (SAC) to bases in England.

Berlin had become the focal point of East-West confrontation and when surface entry into the city was cut by the Soviets, the Allies countered with the now famous Berlin Airlift. To counter further moves by the Communists, SAC deployed sixty B-29s to the United Kingdom where they were stationed at Royal Air Force bases such as RAF Marham, RAF Waddington, RAF Scampton and RAF Lakenheath.

The B-29s were no strangers to Europe, since the aircraft had been involved in training/goodwill visits to England for a number of years. Three aircraft had visited RAF Marham during the Spring of 1946 and, in November of 1946, six B-29s had deployed to Rhein-Main in Germany. Strategic Air Command B-29s began deploying to Europe on a regular basis during 1947 and during that year, nine aircraft of the 97th Bomb Group were based at Giebelstadt, West Germany, for a thirty day training/goodwill tour.

A Boeing B-29 Superfortress of the 2nd Bomb Group taxies in on the rain soaked ramp at Lakenheath Air Base on 11 August 1948. (G. Pennick)

A number of B-29s of the 97th Bomb Group paid a similar visit to RAF Marham during 1947. These early B-29s carried no group markings and most were overall natural metal, although a few had Flat Black undersurfaces. The aircraft carried standard USAF markings, with buzz numbers in Black on natural metal aircraft and in Yellow on aircraft with Flat Black undersurfaces. Later, B-29s began carrying geometric symbols painted on the fin, usually surrounding a Group identification letter.

These symbols, usually a triangle, square, circle or diamond, identified the numbered air force that the aircraft belonged to, while the letter code denoted the group or wing. One of the first Groups to arrive in England for a ninety day tour was the 28th Bomb Group which deployed from Rapid City AFB, South Dakota, to RAF Scampton during 1948. 28th BG aircraft carried a Black R within a Black circle on both sides of the fin. The R denoted the Group while the circle identified the parent unit, the 15th Air Force. Many units later carried their parent numbered Air Force unit badge on the base of the fin. These aircraft also had various colored nose wheel doors and fin tips denoting their respective squadrons.

The 2nd Air Force carried a Black square on its B-29s and the 8th Air Force used a triangle. It is believed that when a Group or Wing transferred from one numbered Air Force to another, their identification letter remained the same; however, the numbered air force geometric identification symbol changed.

During this time frame, the B-29s and B-50s often carried colorful personal markings and squadron colors. The squadron colors were usually carried on the nose wheel doors, fin tips and as fuselage bands. Some B-29s retained Flat Black undersurfaces while others carried Red tail sections and outer wing panels, known as Arctic markings, which were used to make the aircraft more visible in the event of a forced landing on snow covered terrain.

During 1949, the 43rd Bomb Group deployed to Britain with the first Boeing B-50s. Earlier, the B-29s had required forward bases for refueling; however, most of the B-50s were equipped with in-flight refueling gear. To refuel the B-50s, the 43rd Group had a squadron of KB-29M tankers (B-29s with no armament and large fuel tanks installed in the bomb bays and fuel transfer gear added). The KB-29s carried the same style markings as the B-50s (diagonal stripes in squadron colors).

The 2nd Bomb Group continued the style of markings used with the earlier B-29s on their B-50s (painted nose wheel doors, fuselage bands and fin tips). Additionally, large squadron badges were carried on the sides of the aircraft nose.

Aircraft of the 93rd Bomb Group carried individual squadron letters on the fuselage sides followed by the last two digits of the aircraft's serial number. The three squadrons within the Group were, the 328th Bomb Squadron (A), the 329th Squadron (C) and the 330th

A B-29A of the 718th Bomb Squadron, 28th Bomb Group is parked on one of the dispersal pads at RAF Scampton during 1948. The aircraft has the nosewheel doors, propeller hubs and fin tip in Red and carries an 8th Air Force badge on the vertical fin.

Squadron (B). By 1954, the use of Bomb Group letter codes and Air Force geometric identification symbols had terminated.

Occasionally, SB-29 rescue aircraft were also seen in the United Kingdom. These aircraft carried their usual rescue markings including a Yellow, outlined in Black, rear fuselage identification band. SB-29 deployments were usually accompanied by an F-13 (RB-29) photo reconnaissance aircraft. These aircraft also carried the Yellow rescue markings and sometimes a Black tail code.

SAC B-29s and B-50s were regular visitors to RAF St Eval in Cornwall, and they regularly participated in static displays at various RAF bases during the Battle of Britain celebrations between 1948 and 1951. During the early 1950s the first B-36 made its debut into the United Kingdom. The first B-36Ds in England were assigned to the 7th Bomb Group which was based at Lakenheath during exercise **OPERATION UK** held in January of 1951. These aircraft were in natural metal with the last three digits of the serial number on the forward fuselage sides and the 8th Air Force badge carried on the base of the fin.

B-36s made regular visits to England for exercises between 1951 and 1959. On one occasion, an RB-36H (51-5744) of the 72nd Bomb Wing was making a fly-by during RAF St Mawgan's Battle of Britain display (September of 1952), when it developed engine trouble. The aircraft landed, giving the crowd an opportunity to closely inspect a SAC B-36. The aircraft was natural metal with a large Black triangle and S letter code on the fin. The last three digits of the serial were positioned on the forward fuselage sides, the fin tip was Black and the nose wheel doors were Black with a diagonal White stripe.

This B-50A was named *LUCKY LADY II* and was assigned to the 63rd Bomb Squadron, 43rd Bomb Group. The aircraft deployed to Sculthorpe, Norfolk, during August of 1949. (B. Kemp)

The 42nd Bomb Wing visited Upper Heyford and Burtonwood between 15 and 23 September 1954 and later the entire wing deployed to Upper Heyford (October/November 1955). Sixteen B-36s visited Burtonwood in 1956, while Brize Norton also played host to a number of these giants. The B-36s now carried White undersurfaces with the legend U.S. Air Force in Black on the fuselage sides and sometimes the last three digits of the serial number. A Blue Strategic Air Command sash was carried on both sides of the nose with the SAC badge on the port side and the Bomb Wing badge on the starboard side (early aircraft did not always carry the Wing badge).

The first B-47s to visit the United Kingdom arrived on 7 April 1953, when the two aircraft of the 306th Bomb Wing landed at Fairford, Gloucestershire, after flying non-stop from Limestone AFB. After a short visit, they returned to McDill AFB, Florida.

The 306th Bomb Wing, based at McDill AFB, Florida, was the first SAC unit to equip with the B-47B and was the first unit to deploy to the United Kingdom for a ninety day tour of duty. The 306th Bomb Wing commander, COL M. McCoy, arrived at Fairford Air Base on Thursday 4 June 1953 accompanied by fourteen aircraft. A further fifteen B-47s followed over the next two days, bringing the Wing up to its full strength of forty-five aircraft. The 306th BW comprised three squadrons, the 367th, 368th and 369th. Squadron markings consisted of a tail band in the appropriate color and a small squadron badge on the fuselage just below the cockpit. The B-47s remained in USAFE until August/September of 1953.

The 305th Bomb Wing (Medium) was the next Stratojet unit to deploy. The wing, commanded by COL E. Vandevater, Jr., arrived at Fairford in September of 1953 and returned to the U.S. on 3 December 1953. The wing had been accompanied during its deployment by KC-97 tankers, which were also based in England during the bomber's ninety day tour of duty and carried out air-to-air refueling of the B-47s both on the trip to England and on their return to the States. The refueling squadrons were normally assigned to the particular bomb wing for the entire period of their deployment. The tankers were usually overall natural metal with a band on the fin in the squadron color and Arctic Red outer wing panels and tail sections. The 22nd Bomb Wing followed and was based at Upper Heyford from December of 1953 until March of 1954.

A Boeing B-50D of the 328th Bomb Squadron, 93rd Bomb Group, 15th Air Force flies over England during a Group deployment during the Summer of 1950.

The B-47s were usually overall natural metal. Later, they were painted with a White anti-nuclear flash paint scheme. The White area included the undersides of the wings, tails, engine nacelles and fuselage, with the White area running halfway up the fuselage side. Wing/squadron assignment was usually indicated by a colored stripe (sometimes two) applied horizontally or diagonally across the top of the fin. A small U.S. Air Force legend was applied to the upper forward fuselage sides between the cockpit and the White demarcation line. The SAC sash was carried on each side of the nose with the wing insignia on the starboard side and the SAC badge on the port side. The auxiliary fuel tanks were usually natural metal.

The 97th Bomb Wing deployed with their B-47Es to RAF Upper Heyford from May to July of 1956 together with the KC-97s of the 97th ARS. The B-47Es had a slightly revised anti-nuclear paint scheme, with the White area being reduced.

Other Bomb Wings that rotated through English bases included the 98th Bomb Wing at Lakenheath (November of 1955 - January of 1956) and the 310th Wing at Greenham Common (October of 1956 - January of 1957).

During 1958 the Air Force changed its policy of bomber deployments. The ninety day deployments were replaced by twenty-one

This KB-29P, parked on the ramp at Prestwick, Scotland, during 1952, was assigned to the 97th Air Refueling Squadron. The aircraft carries the Group badge on the nose and has the nosewheel doors, propeller hubs and fin tip in Red. (MAP)

day deployments of aircraft and crews instead of entire bomber wings. This method of bomber deployment lasted until 1965. Besides B-47E bombers, English bases also played host to the RB-47Es, EB-47s and RB-47Hs of the 55th Strategic Reconnaissance Wing.

Stratojets were based at Brize Norton, Fairford, Greenham Common, and Mildenhall. SAC units using these bases included the 98th, 307th and 310th Bomb Wings (Greenham Common) and the 2nd, 308th and 384th Bomb Wings (Fairford). The 100th, 301st and 98th also used Bruntingthorpe, Chelveston and Upper Heyford for short periods.

Other units known to have operated in England were the 301st and 380th Wings with EB-47s at Brize Norton, the 340th Wing at Fairford with B-47Es, and the 96th and 307th Wings at Upper Heyford.

The 93rd Bomb Wing at Castle AFB, California, had been serving as the Combat Crew Training Unit for the B-47 when it was selected to become the B-52 Combat Crew Training Wing, receiving its first aircraft during mid-1955. The 93rd made a number of record flights with the B-52, including the first non-stop jet flight around the world during January of 1957. Five B-52Bs took off from Castle AFB to participate in the record attempt. Three aircraft completed the 23,574 miles trip in an average time of 45.19 hours. Two aircraft diverted, with one landing in Newfoundland and the other at Brize Norton. This aircraft, a B-52B (53-395) named *City of Turlock* was assigned to the 330th Bomb Squadron. It was the first B-52 to arrive in England although later the B-52s became regular visitors to the United Kingdom, turning up at bases such as Greenham Common and also taking part in RAF Bomber competitions.

(Above) *HOMOGENIZED ETHYL* was a KB-29M of the 43rd Air Refueling Squadron which was assigned to the 43rd Bomb Group, 15th Air Force. The squadron carried its code letter, circle K, on the fin in Black and a 15th Air Force badge just in front of the code letter. (D. Menard)

(Below) A Boeing B-47E Stratojet of the 97th Bomb Wing parked on the ramp during Upper Heyford's Armed Forces Day Display, held during May of 1956. This particular aircraft later took part in the Zurich Air Show, at Zurich, Switzerland. (Robinson)

(Below) This B-52B was named *City of Turlock* and was the first B-52 to visit the United Kingdom. The aircraft was assigned to the 330th Bomb Squadron, 93rd Bomb Wing and deployed to RAF Brize Norton, on 18 January 1957. (Robinson)

10th TACTICAL RECONNAISSANCE WING

The 10th Tactical Reconnaissance Group (10th TRG) was reactivated in July of 1952 as part of the United States Air Forces Europe (USAFE) and based at Toul-Rosieres, France, where it absorbed the aircraft and personnel of the 117th TRG. The Group then moved to Spangdahlem Air Base, Germany, where it was stationed from May of 1953 until August of 1959. During this time period, the Group was redesignated the 10th Tactical Reconnaissance Wing (10th TRW).

The Wing consisted of the following squadrons: the 1st TRS equipped with RB-26s (later RB-57A/Cs), the 32nd TRS equipped with RF-80s and RF-84Fs, the 38th TRS with RF-80s and RF-84Fs and the 42nd TRS with T-33As and RB-26s. Squadron colors were Black and White (1st TRS), Red and Yellow (32nd TRS), Green and Yellow (38th TRS) and Red and White (42nd TRS). The Air Force, to make better use of maintenance, training, and supply assets, decided to reorganize both the 10th TRW and 66th TRW to standardize their equipment. Up to this time each wing had squadrons operating different aircraft types. After the reorganization (which shifted squadrons between the wings), the 10th TRW was standardized on the RB-66 and the 66th TRW flew the RF-84F.

The squadrons shifted to the 10th TRW from the 66th TRW were as follows: the 19th TRS (RB-66Bs) in January of 1958 and the 30th TRS (RB-66Bs) also during 1958. The 1st TRW had converted to the RB-66B during December of 1957, while the Wing's fourth squadron, the 42nd TRS, was re-equipped with the RB-66C during 1957. The main difference between the RB-66B and RB-66C was the wing tip pods and external fuel tanks carried by the RB-66C.

The 66th TRW received the 32nd TRS and 38th TRS, both equipped with the Republic RF-84F. They joined the two RF-84F squadrons already serving with the 66th TRW (302nd and 303rd TRS), completing the reorganization.

In August of 1959, the 10th Wing relocated to three airfields in England. The Wing Headquarters was based at RAF Alconbury, Huntingdonshire, along with the 1st and 30th TRS. RAF Bruntingthorpe became home base for the 19 TRS and RAF Chelveston housed the Weather and Reconnaissance unit, the 42nd TRS.

Squadron markings consisted of a band (in squadron color) carried diagonally across the engine nacelle as follows: Blue (1st TRS), Green (19th TRS), Yellow (30th TRS), Red (42nd TRS). The aircraft carried large Wing badges on the fuselage sides and a Black comet (star) with a Red, Yellow, Blue and Green plume was positioned just above the rudder on the vertical fin.

One RB-66 (54-459) had quite a history. It arrived at Spangdahlem Air Base, Germany, on 28 November 1956, the first RB-66C to serve outside the United States. Assigned to the 42nd TRS, the aircraft was named *Kries Wittlich* by the mayor of the town near the base in formal ceremonies on Armed Forces Day of 1957. To commemorate the event, the coat of arms of the town was painted on the port side of the fuselage below the cockpit.

The aircraft served with the 42nd TRS through the unit's move to RAF Chelveston and during July 1962 it returned to the continent when the 42nd relocated to Toul-Rosieres Air Base, France. During July of 1965, *Kreis Wittlich* moved to Chamberly Air Base, France, when the 42nd was reassigned to the newly created 26th TRW.

During March of 1966, the aircraft left Europe for overhaul in the U.S. and deployment to South East Asia. After a second overhaul and modification, she returned to Europe during April of 1970, now designated as an EB-66C serving with the 39th Tactical Electronic Warfare Squadron, based at Spangdahlem, Germany.

Shortly after the 10th Wing moved to England, its aircraft began a modification program which replaced the tail guns with an ECM housing (the modification did not change the aircraft designation). Later, some fourteen RB-66Bs of the 47th Bomb Wing were modified to RB-66C standards and operated by the 42nd TRS at RAF Chelveston. This program also included three aircraft which were redesignated as EB-66Bs. As a result of the various modification programs, the 10th TRW operated three RB-66 variants: RB-66Bs (1st, 19th and 30th TRS) and RB-66Cs and EB-66Bs with the 42nd TRS.

During 1960 the engine nacelle stripes were removed, as was the large wing badge on the fuselage; however, the Black shooting star and plume on the fin was retained. A new marking, in the form of a geometric symbol, was carried on the fuselage speed brake. An aircraft might carry a diamond or triangle in its squadron color, although the marking was not carried on all aircraft within the Wing. The purpose of the marking is believed to have been maintenance related. The 10th TRW retained its RB-66s until replaced by the RF-4C Phantom II during 1965.

(Above) This RB-66B, assigned to the 30th TRS, 10th TRW on the ramp at Prestwick, Scotland, during May of 1960, retains its twin 20mm cannon tail armament. The national insignia is oversized and the aircraft carries a broad Yellow stripe on the engine nacelle. (MAP)

(Below) An RB-66C of the 42nd TRS parked on the ramp at Chelveston on Armed Forces Day Display (28 May) 1960. This aircraft carries a small sized national insignia and has the wing tip ECM pods covered. (D. Menard)

(Below) An overall Black Douglas A-26B Invader of the 38th Bomb Group based at Laon, France, during 1954. The Invader's squadron assignment and the color of the tail band are unknown. (Robinson)

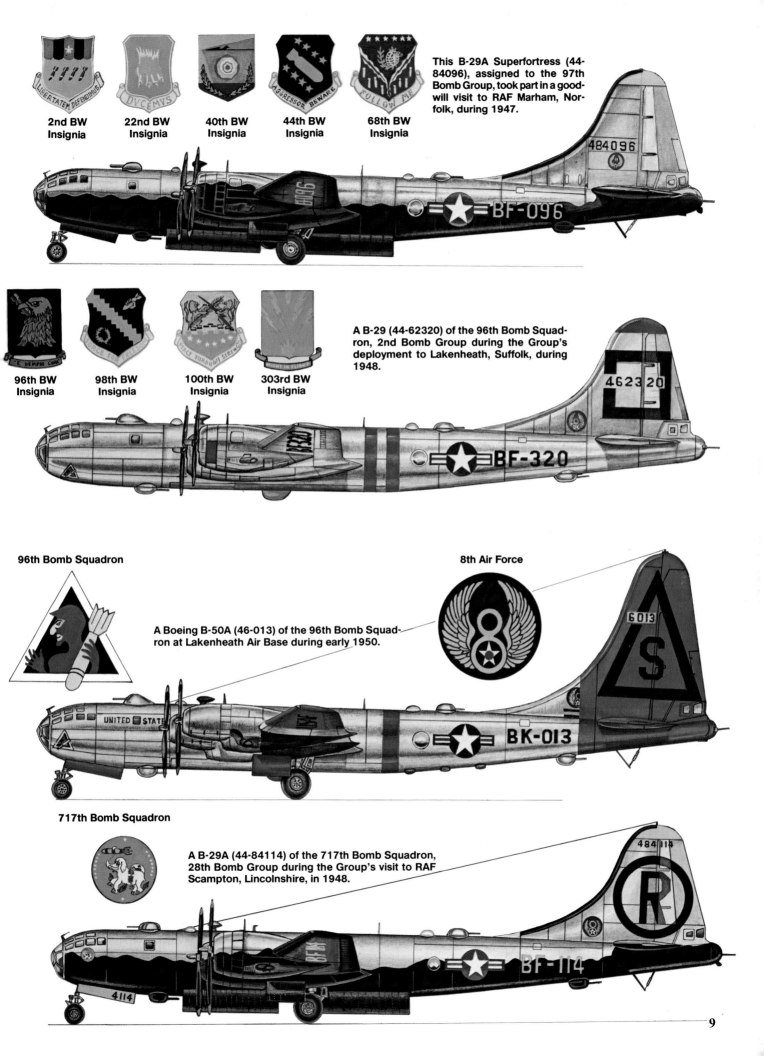

2nd BW
Insignia

22nd BW
Insignia

40th BW
Insignia

44th BW
Insignia

68th BW
Insignia

This B-29A Superfortress (44-84096), assigned to the 97th Bomb Group, took part in a good-will visit to RAF Marham, Norfolk, during 1947.

96th BW
Insignia

98th BW
Insignia

100th BW
Insignia

303rd BW
Insignia

A B-29 (44-62320) of the 96th Bomb Squadron, 2nd Bomb Group during the Group's deployment to Lakenheath, Suffolk, during 1948.

96th Bomb Squadron

8th Air Force

A Boeing B-50A (46-013) of the 96th Bomb Squadron at Lakenheath Air Base during early 1950.

717th Bomb Squadron

A B-29A (44-84114) of the 717th Bomb Squadron, 28th Bomb Group during the Group's visit to RAF Scampton, Lincolnshire, in 1948.

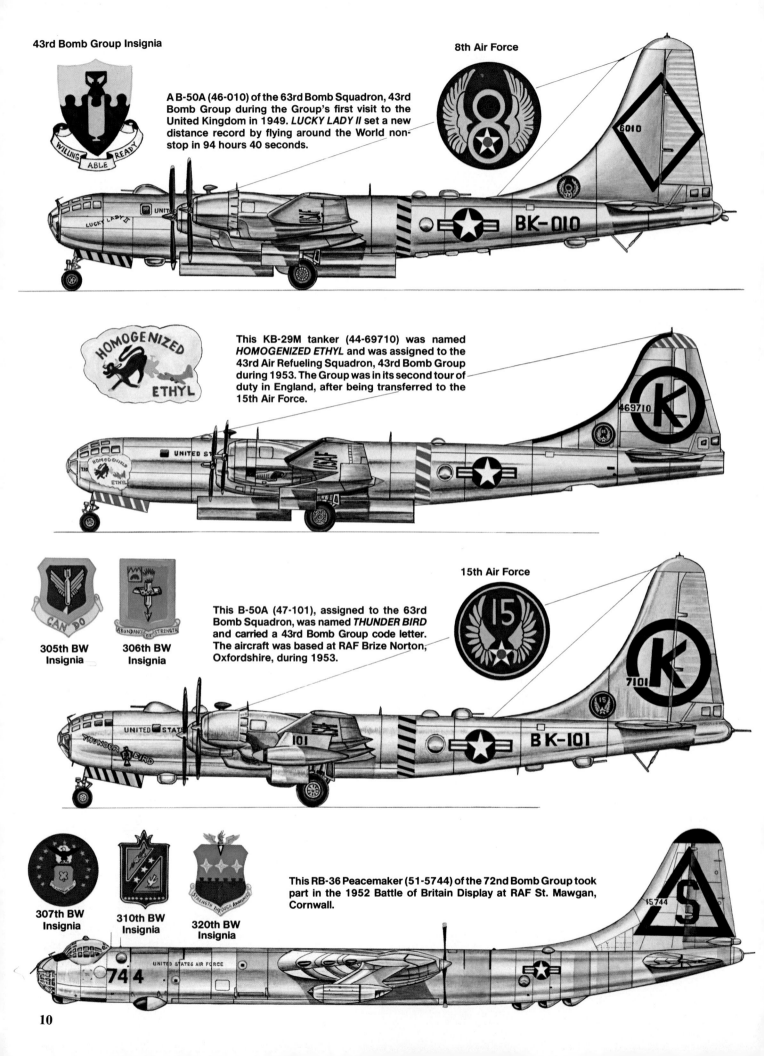

43rd Bomb Group Insignia

WILLING ABLE READY

8th Air Force

A B-50A (46-010) of the 63rd Bomb Squadron, 43rd Bomb Group during the Group's first visit to the United Kingdom in 1949. *LUCKY LADY II* set a new distance record by flying around the World non-stop in 94 hours 40 seconds.

HOMOGENIZED ETHYL

This KB-29M tanker (44-69710) was named *HOMOGENIZED ETHYL* and was assigned to the 43rd Air Refueling Squadron, 43rd Bomb Group during 1953. The Group was in its second tour of duty in England, after being transferred to the 15th Air Force.

305th BW Insignia

CAN DO

306th BW Insignia

ABUNDANCE OF STRENGTH

15th Air Force

This B-50A (47-101), assigned to the 63rd Bomb Squadron, was named *THUNDER BIRD* and carried a 43rd Bomb Group code letter. The aircraft was based at RAF Brize Norton, Oxfordshire, during 1953.

307th BW Insignia

310th BW Insignia

320th BW Insignia

STRENGTH THROUGH AWARENESS

This RB-36 Peacemaker (51-5744) of the 72nd Bomb Group took part in the 1952 Battle of Britain Display at RAF St. Mawgan, Cornwall.

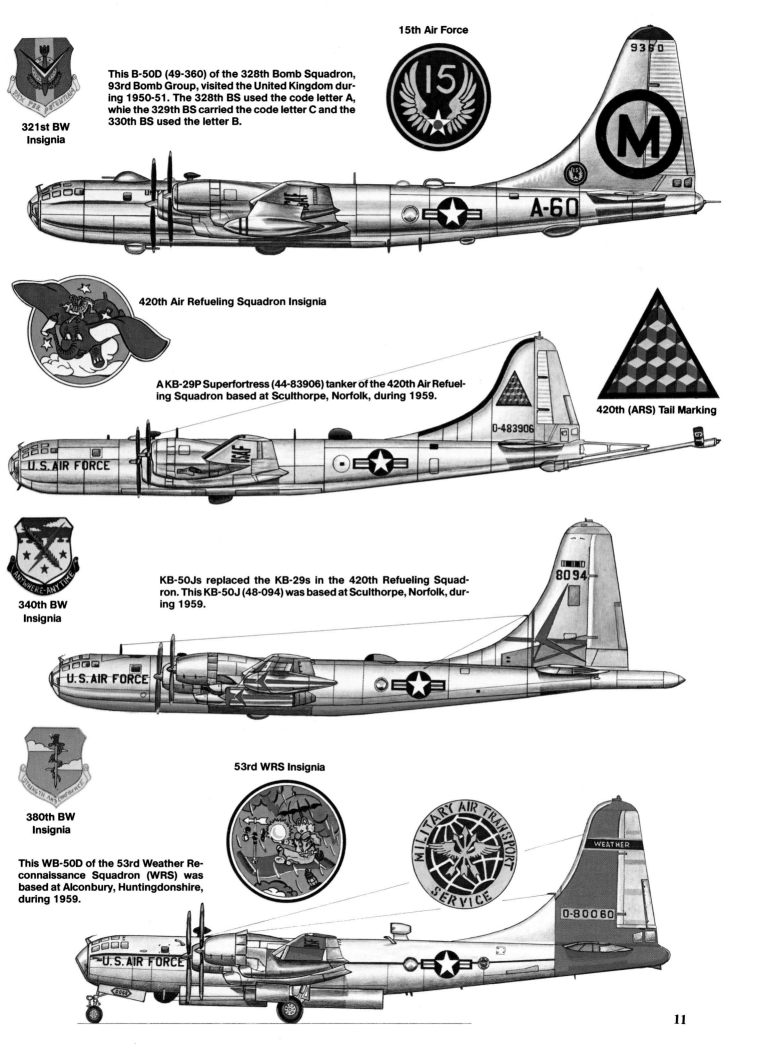

321st BW Insignia

This B-50D (49-360) of the 328th Bomb Squadron, 93rd Bomb Group, visited the United Kingdom during 1950-51. The 328th BS used the code letter A, while the 329th BS carried the code letter C and the 330th BS used the letter B.

15th Air Force

420th Air Refueling Squadron Insignia

A KB-29P Superfortress (44-83906) tanker of the 420th Air Refueling Squadron based at Sculthorpe, Norfolk, during 1959.

420th (ARS) Tail Marking

340th BW Insignia

KB-50Js replaced the KB-29s in the 420th Refueling Squadron. This KB-50J (48-094) was based at Sculthorpe, Norfolk, during 1959.

380th BW Insignia

53rd WRS Insignia

This WB-50D of the 53rd Weather Reconnaissance Squadron (WRS) was based at Alconbury, Huntingdonshire, during 1959.

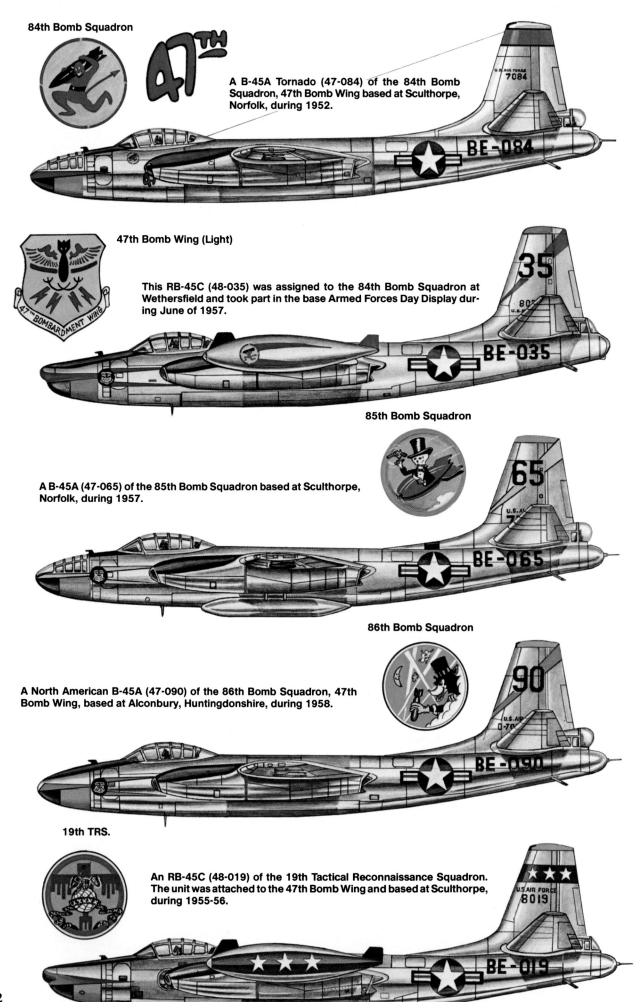

84th Bomb Squadron

A B-45A Tornado (47-084) of the 84th Bomb Squadron, 47th Bomb Wing based at Sculthorpe, Norfolk, during 1952.

47th Bomb Wing (Light)

This RB-45C (48-035) was assigned to the 84th Bomb Squadron at Wethersfield and took part in the base Armed Forces Day Display during June of 1957.

85th Bomb Squadron

A B-45A (47-065) of the 85th Bomb Squadron based at Sculthorpe, Norfolk, during 1957.

86th Bomb Squadron

A North American B-45A (47-090) of the 86th Bomb Squadron, 47th Bomb Wing, based at Alconbury, Huntingdonshire, during 1958.

19th TRS.

An RB-45C (48-019) of the 19th Tactical Reconnaissance Squadron. The unit was attached to the 47th Bomb Wing and based at Sculthorpe, during 1955-56.

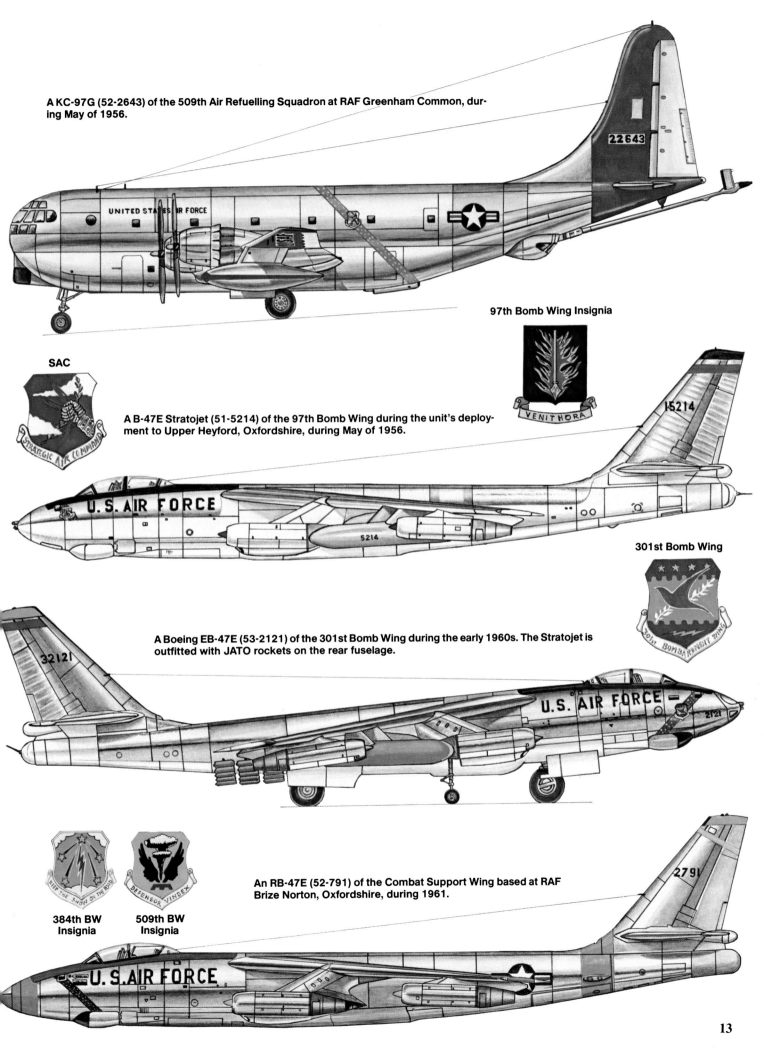

A KC-97G (52-2643) of the 509th Air Refuelling Squadron at RAF Greenham Common, during May of 1956.

97th Bomb Wing Insignia

SAC

A B-47E Stratojet (51-5214) of the 97th Bomb Wing during the unit's deployment to Upper Heyford, Oxfordshire, during May of 1956.

301st Bomb Wing

A Boeing EB-47E (53-2121) of the 301st Bomb Wing during the early 1960s. The Stratojet is outfitted with JATO rockets on the rear fuselage.

384th BW Insignia

509th BW Insignia

An RB-47E (52-791) of the Combat Support Wing based at RAF Brize Norton, Oxfordshire, during 1961.

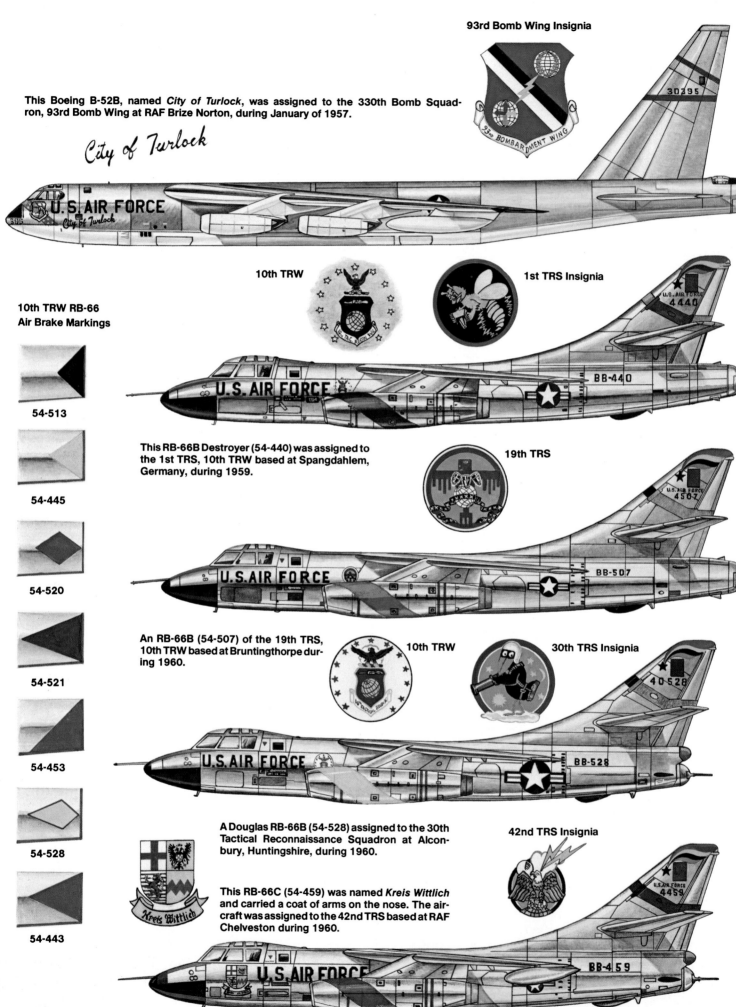

93rd Bomb Wing Insignia

This Boeing B-52B, named *City of Turlock*, was assigned to the 330th Bomb Squadron, 93rd Bomb Wing at RAF Brize Norton, during January of 1957.

City of Turlock

30395

U.S. AIR FORCE
City of Turlock

10th TRW

1st TRS Insignia

U.S. AIR FORCE

4440

BB-440

10th TRW RB-66 Air Brake Markings

54-513

54-445

54-520

54-521

54-453

54-528

54-443

This RB-66B Destroyer (54-440) was assigned to the 1st TRS, 10th TRW based at Spangdahlem, Germany, during 1959.

19th TRS

U.S. AIR FORCE

4507

BB-507

An RB-66B (54-507) of the 19th TRS, 10th TRW based at Bruntingthorpe during 1960.

10th TRW

30th TRS Insignia

U.S. AIR FORCE

40528

BB-528

A Douglas RB-66B (54-528) assigned to the 30th Tactical Reconnaissance Squadron at Alconbury, Huntingshire, during 1960.

Kreis Wittlich

This RB-66C (54-459) was named *Kreis Wittlich* and carried a coat of arms on the nose. The aircraft was assigned to the 42nd TRS based at RAF Chelveston during 1960.

42nd TRS Insignia

U.S. AIR FORCE

4459

BB-459

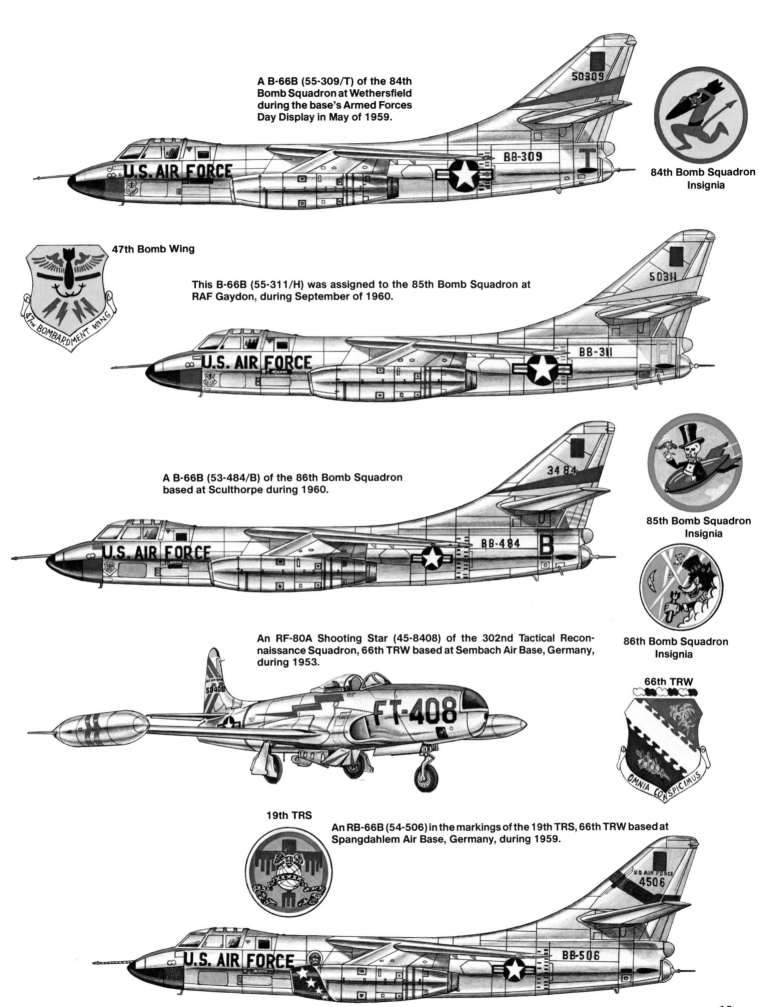

A B-66B (55-309/T) of the 84th Bomb Squadron at Wethersfield during the base's Armed Forces Day Display in May of 1959.

84th Bomb Squadron Insignia

47th Bomb Wing

This B-66B (55-311/H) was assigned to the 85th Bomb Squadron at RAF Gaydon, during September of 1960.

A B-66B (53-484/B) of the 86th Bomb Squadron based at Sculthorpe during 1960.

85th Bomb Squadron Insignia

86th Bomb Squadron Insignia

An RF-80A Shooting Star (45-8408) of the 302nd Tactical Reconnaissance Squadron, 66th TRW based at Sembach Air Base, Germany, during 1953.

66th TRW

19th TRS

An RB-66B (54-506) in the markings of the 19th TRS, 66th TRW based at Spangdahlem Air Base, Germany, during 1959.

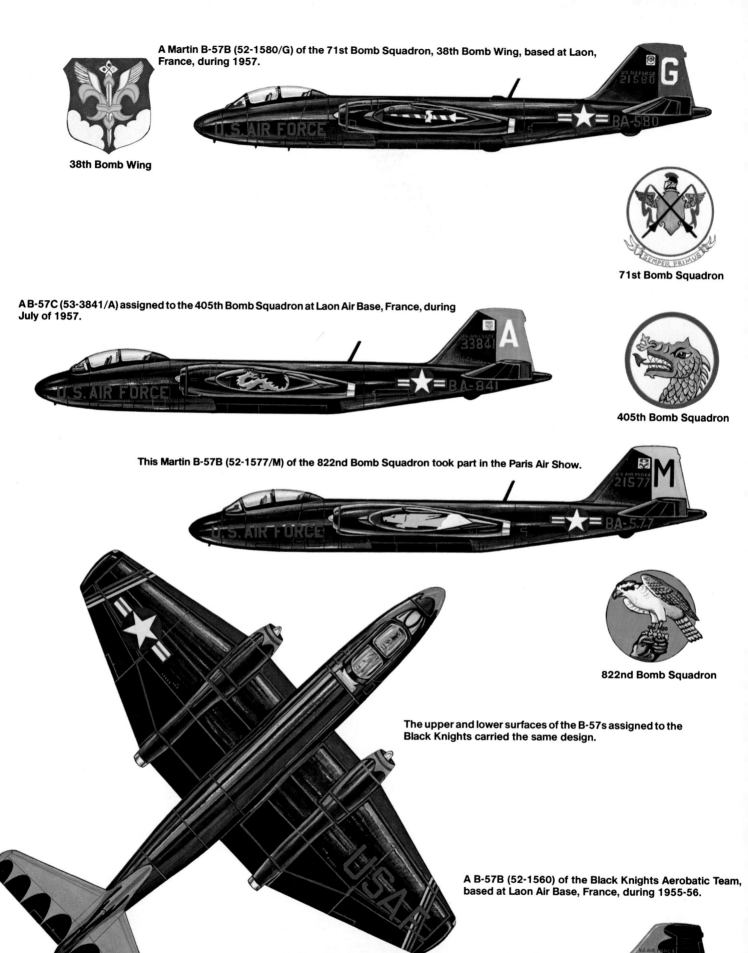

A Martin B-57B (52-1580/G) of the 71st Bomb Squadron, 38th Bomb Wing, based at Laon, France, during 1957.

38th Bomb Wing

71st Bomb Squadron

A B-57C (53-3841/A) assigned to the 405th Bomb Squadron at Laon Air Base, France, during July of 1957.

405th Bomb Squadron

This Martin B-57B (52-1577/M) of the 822nd Bomb Squadron took part in the Paris Air Show.

822nd Bomb Squadron

The upper and lower surfaces of the B-57s assigned to the Black Knights carried the same design.

A B-57B (52-1560) of the Black Knights Aerobatic Team, based at Laon Air Base, France, during 1955-56.

An RB-57A (52-1495) of the 1st TRS,10th TRW, based at Spangdahlem, Germany, during 1955.

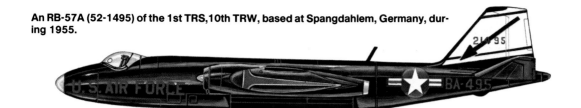

A Republic RF-84F (51-17005) of the 30th Tactical Reconnaissance Squadron, 10th TRW, based at Spangdahlem, Germany, during 1956, before being moved to the 66th TRW.

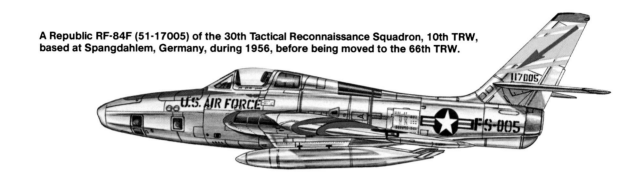

An RB-57A (52-1456) of the 30th Tactical Reconnaissance Squadron, 66th TRW stationed at Sembach Air Base, Germany, during 1955-56.

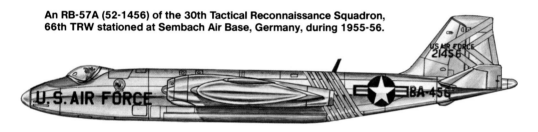

66th TRW

30th TRS

This RB-57A (52-1456) of the 30th TRS, carries later style markings and Yellow exercise bands. The aircraft was based at Sembach, during 1956-57.

The lead RF-84F (51-1894) was assigned to the 303rd TRS and flown by the commander of the 66th TRW. His wingman (51-1933) was a flight leader with the 303rd TRS.

17

An RF-84F (52-7292) of the 32nd Tactical Reconnaissance Squadron, 66th TRW based at Phalsbourg Air Base, France, during 1958.

66th Tactical Reconnaissance Wing

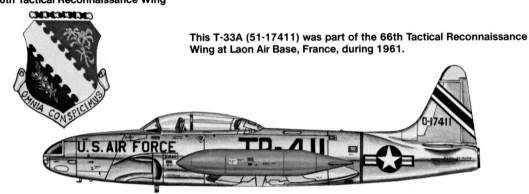

This T-33A (51-17411) was part of the 66th Tactical Reconnaissance Wing at Laon Air Base, France, during 1961.

This Shooting Star (51-17411) carries later style markings used by the 66th Tactical Reconnaissance Wing during 1962.

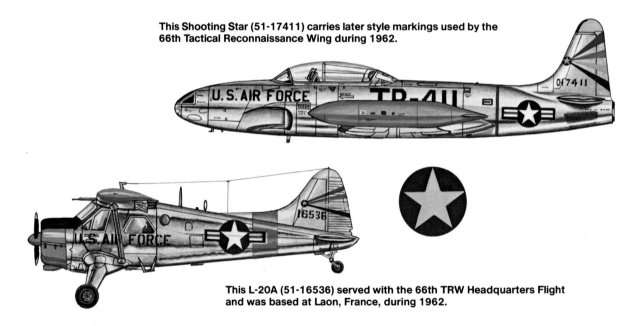

This L-20A (51-16536) served with the 66th TRW Headquarters Flight and was based at Laon, France, during 1962.

This C-47A (42-102710) was assigned to the 66th TRW Headquarters Flight, based at Sembach, Germany, during 1956.

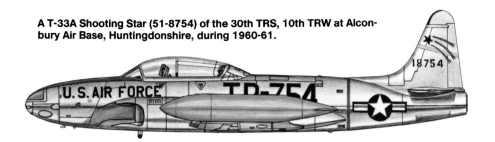

A T-33A Shooting Star (51-8754) of the 30th TRS, 10th TRW at Alconbury Air Base, Huntingdonshire, during 1960-61.

10th TRW

This Lockheed T-33A Shooting Star (52-9624) carried revised 10th TRW markings during 1962. The unit was based at Alconbury, Huntingdonshire.

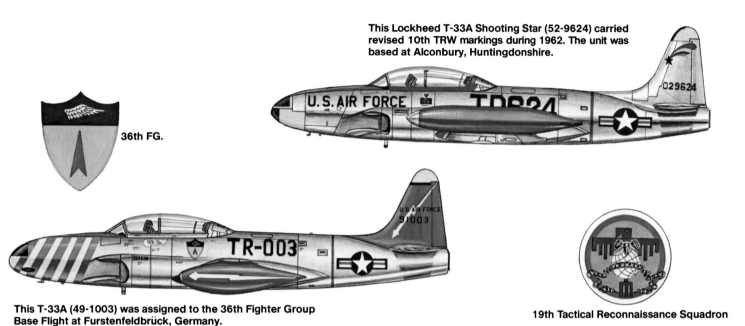

36th FG.

This T-33A (49-1003) was assigned to the 36th Fighter Group Base Flight at Furstenfeldbrück, Germany.

19th Tactical Reconnaissance Squadron

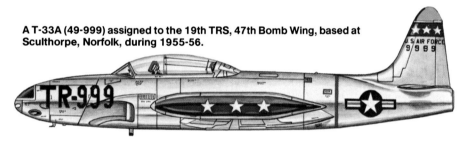

A T-33A (49-999) assigned to the 19th TRS, 47th Bomb Wing, based at Sculthorpe, Norfolk, during 1955-56.

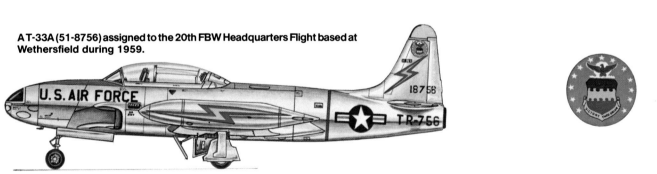

A T-33A (51-8756) assigned to the 20th FBW Headquarters Flight based at Wethersfield during 1959.

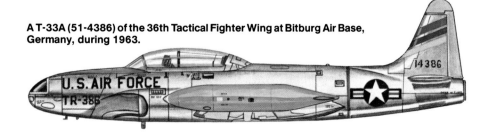

A T-33A (51-4386) of the 36th Tactical Fighter Wing at Bitburg Air Base, Germany, during 1963.

A T-33A (51-6876) of the 50th Wing Headquarters Flight at Hahn Air Base, Germany, during 1959.

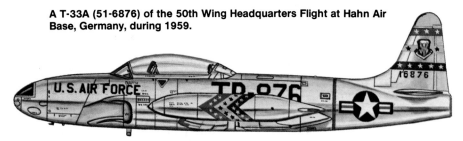

431st FIS Insignia

The 431st FIS used this T-33A (52-9833) while stationed at Zaragoza Air Base, Spain, during 1962.

T-33As like this Shooting Star (51-4474) of the 514th FIS, 406th FIG were widely used as hacks. This T-33 was based at Manston, Kent, during 1957.

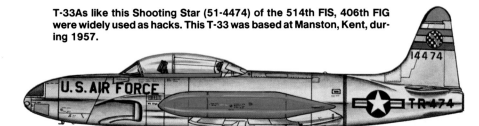

A Lockheed T-33A (51-4383) of the 7101st Air Base Wing at Wiesbaden, Germany, during 1960.

7272nd FTW

A T-33A Shooting Star (53-5824) assigned to the 7272nd Flying Training Wing, based at Wheelus Air Base, Libya, during 1962.

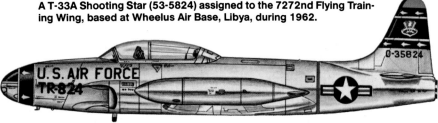

A T-33A (53-1544) assigned to the 81st Fighter Bomber Wing Base Flight at Bentwaters, Suffolk, during 1957.

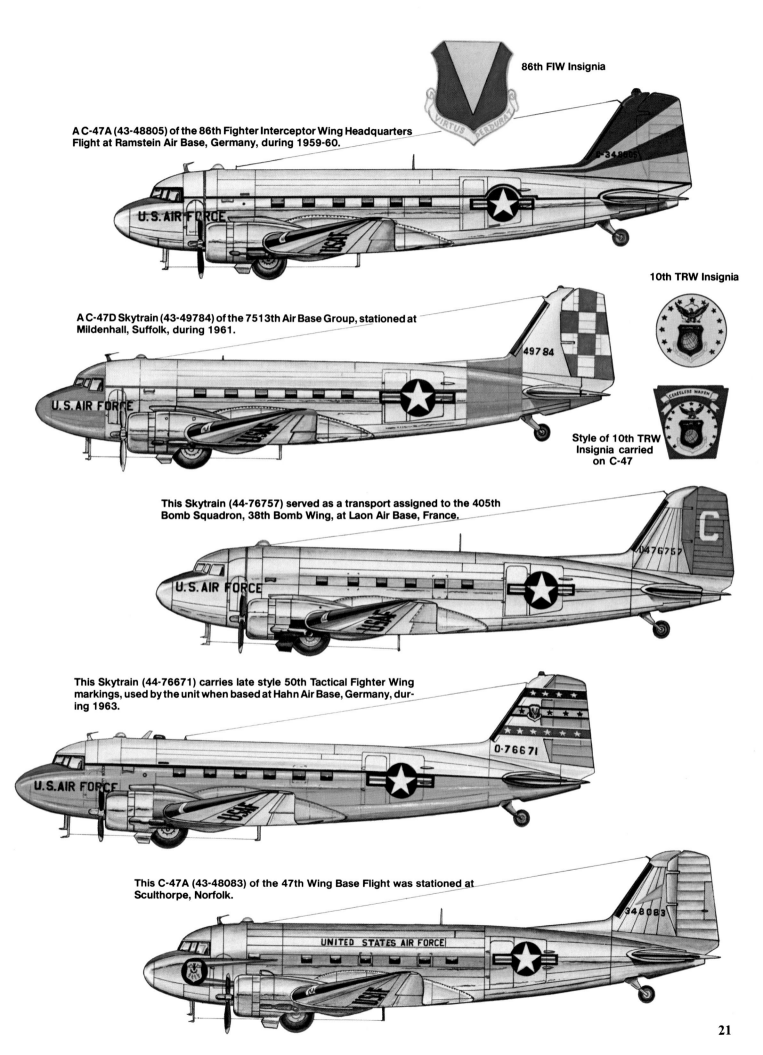

86th FIW Insignia

VIRTUS PERDURAT

A C-47A (43-48805) of the 86th Fighter Interceptor Wing Headquarters Flight at Ramstein Air Base, Germany, during 1959-60.

O-348805

U.S. AIR FORCE

USAF

10th TRW Insignia

A C-47D Skytrain (43-49784) of the 7513th Air Base Group, stationed at Mildenhall, Suffolk, during 1961.

49784

U.S. AIR FORCE

USAF

CEASELESS WATCH

Style of 10th TRW Insignia carried on C-47

This Skytrain (44-76757) served as a transport assigned to the 405th Bomb Squadron, 38th Bomb Wing, at Laon Air Base, France.

C

O476757

U.S. AIR FORCE

USAF

This Skytrain (44-76671) carries late style 50th Tactical Fighter Wing markings, used by the unit when based at Hahn Air Base, Germany, during 1963.

O-76671

U.S. AIR FORCE

USAF

This C-47A (43-48083) of the 47th Wing Base Flight was stationed at Sculthorpe, Norfolk.

348083

UNITED STATES AIR FORCE

USAF

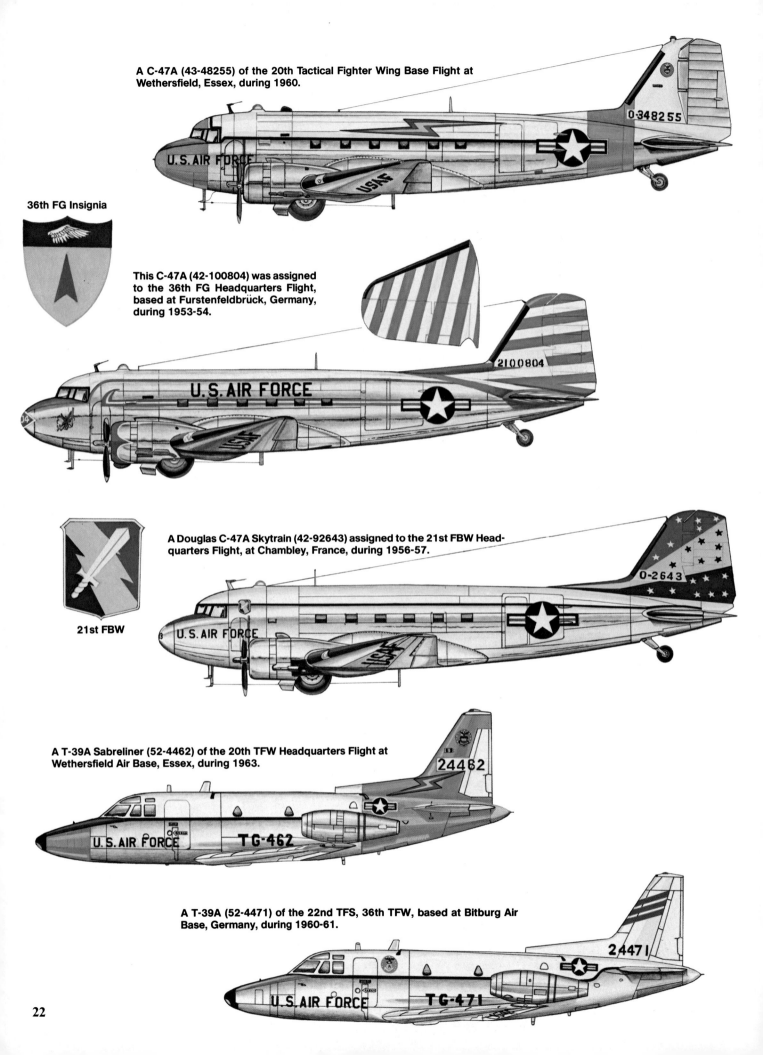

A C-47A (43-48255) of the 20th Tactical Fighter Wing Base Flight at Wethersfield, Essex, during 1960.

36th FG Insignia

This C-47A (42-100804) was assigned to the 36th FG Headquarters Flight, based at Furstenfeldbrück, Germany, during 1953-54.

A Douglas C-47A Skytrain (42-92643) assigned to the 21st FBW Headquarters Flight, at Chambley, France, during 1956-57.

21st FBW

A T-39A Sabreliner (52-4462) of the 20th TFW Headquarters Flight at Wethersfield Air Base, Essex, during 1963.

A T-39A (52-4471) of the 22nd TFS, 36th TFW, based at Bitburg Air Base, Germany, during 1960-61.

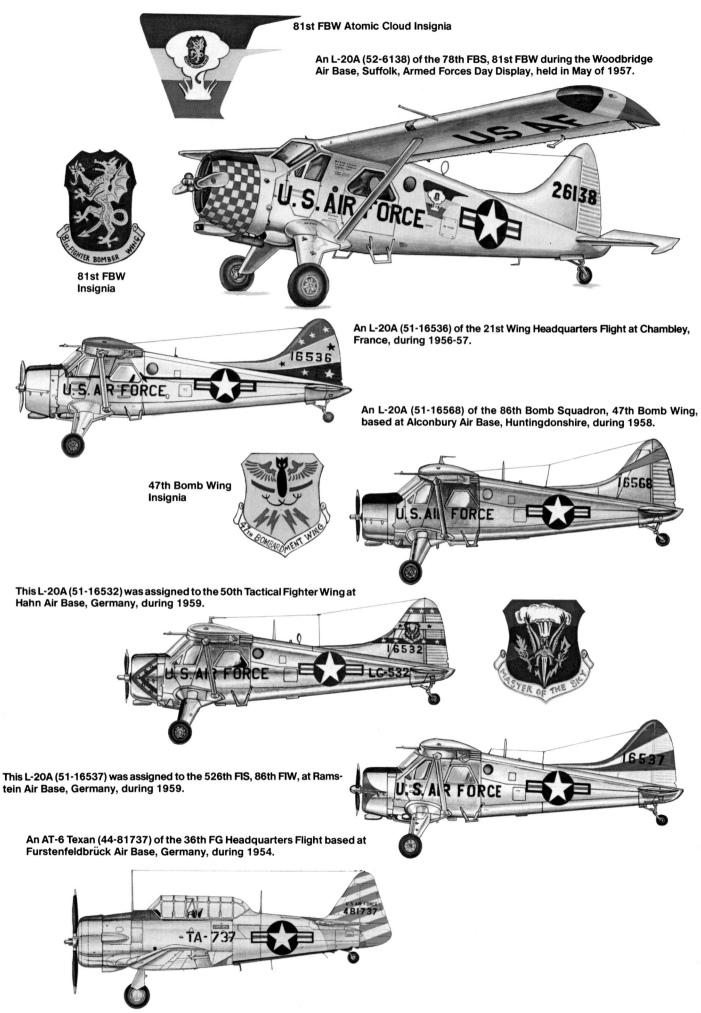

81st FBW Atomic Cloud Insignia

An L-20A (52-6138) of the 78th FBS, 81st FBW during the Woodbridge Air Base, Suffolk, Armed Forces Day Display, held in May of 1957.

81st FBW Insignia

An L-20A (51-16536) of the 21st Wing Headquarters Flight at Chambley, France, during 1956-57.

An L-20A (51-16568) of the 86th Bomb Squadron, 47th Bomb Wing, based at Alconbury Air Base, Huntingdonshire, during 1958.

47th Bomb Wing Insignia

This L-20A (51-16532) was assigned to the 50th Tactical Fighter Wing at Hahn Air Base, Germany, during 1959.

This L-20A (51-16537) was assigned to the 526th FIS, 86th FIW, at Ramstein Air Base, Germany, during 1959.

An AT-6 Texan (44-81737) of the 36th FG Headquarters Flight based at Furstenfeldbrück Air Base, Germany, during 1954.

23

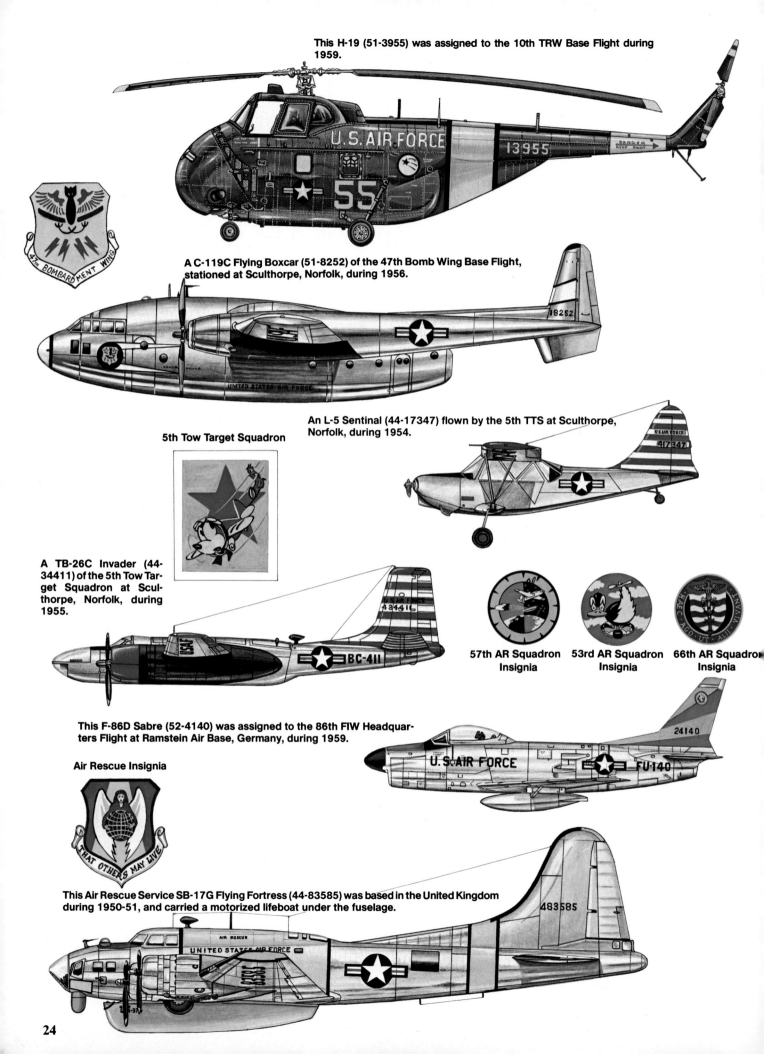

This H-19 (51-3955) was assigned to the 10th TRW Base Flight during 1959.

A C-119C Flying Boxcar (51-8252) of the 47th Bomb Wing Base Flight, stationed at Sculthorpe, Norfolk, during 1956.

5th Tow Target Squadron

An L-5 Sentinal (44-17347) flown by the 5th TTS at Sculthorpe, Norfolk, during 1954.

A TB-26C Invader (44-34411) of the 5th Tow Target Squadron at Sculthorpe, Norfolk, during 1955.

57th AR Squadron Insignia

53rd AR Squadron Insignia

66th AR Squadron Insignia

This F-86D Sabre (52-4140) was assigned to the 86th FIW Headquarters Flight at Ramstein Air Base, Germany, during 1959.

Air Rescue Insignia

This Air Rescue Service SB-17G Flying Fortress (44-83585) was based in the United Kingdom during 1950-51, and carried a motorized lifeboat under the fuselage.

38th BOMBARDMENT WING (LIGHT)

During May of 1952, the first Douglas B-26 Invaders arrived at Laon Air Base, France. These aircraft were part of the 126th Light Bomb Wing, an Air National Guard Unit with squadrons originating from Chicago, Illinois and Joplin, Missouri. On 1 January 1953, the 126th Wing was redesignated as the 38th Bomb Group (Light) with three squadrons. The squadrons and their identification colors were 71st BS (Red), 405th BS (Green) and the 822nd BS (Yellow). The B-26s carried their squadron color in a band across the vertical fin, with a large individual aircraft letter over it.

During 1955, the B-26s were replaced by Martin B-57s, with the first five B-57Bs being ferried from Warner-Robbins AFB, Georgia, led by the Group Commander, COL B. Taylor. These aircraft were overall Gloss Black with the tip of the vertical fin in their respective squadron color. Later, more colorful markings were carried, with the entire rudder being painted in the squadron color along with an individual aircraft letter. The rudder/letter colors were: Red/ White letter (71st BS), Green/White letter (405th BS) and Yellow/Black letter (822nd BS). It is thought that each squadron carried the identification letters commencing with A and moving through the alphabet. Two 71st Squadron and two 822nd Squadron aircraft were noted during the same period, both carrying the letter D and G. How many aircraft were assigned to each squadron is unknown, but one 405th Squadron aircraft carried the letter O, while an 822nd Squadron aircraft was seen carrying a P, indicating a possible unit strength of sixteen aircraft.

All aircraft carried the 38th Wing Badge high on both sides of the tail, while the squadron insignia was carried on wing tip tanks. The 71st BS carried a Red and White Lance and Knight's helmet, the 405th BS carried a Green Dragon and the 822nd BS had a Yellow Hawk and White Cloud on the tank.

The 38th Bomb Wing was unique in having the only Medium Bomber Aerobatic Team in the Air Force. The team, known as the Black Knights, was formed with pilots from the 71st and 822nd BS under the leadership of MAJ C. Jackson, the Operation Officer of the 71st Bomb Squadron. During this time the USAFE already had one authorized aerobatic team, the Skyblazers. This team was formed with pilots from the 48th Tactical Fighter Wing at Chaumont Air Base, France, flying Red, White and Blue F-86F Sabres.

The Black Knights team consisted of five B-57s and their pilots, drawn from the three squadrons (although initially the team was started with crews from the 71st Squadron). The aircraft were painted with Bright Orange areas on the nose, engine air intakes, horizontal stabilizers and vertical fin. The squadron colors were painted in bands running diagonally above and below the wings (Red, outboard, Green and Yellow, inboard). Known aircraft serial numbers, pilots and their team positions were as follows:

MAJ C. Jackson (52-1578, lead aircraft)

MAJ W. McDannal (53-3869, left wing)

CAPT J. Harris (52-1560, slot aircraft)

1st LT W. McCord (right wing)

CAPT R. Rush (solo aircraft)

The Black Knights conducted most of their displays at Laon Air Base, although one display was made at Chatereaux Air Base, France. This display was held in bad weather with a low cloud ceiling which restricted the display routines to low level. The most impressive event of the display was a low level, high speed pass by a B-57 flown by CAPT Rush.

Douglas C-47s were also assigned to the squadrons for personnel and cargo transport and carried the colored rudder and an alloted code letter. T-33s assigned for proficiency flying are believed to have carried the lower letters of the alphabet and were assigned to the base flight with their own squadron color.

47th BOMBARDMENT WING (LIGHT)

The 47th Bombardment Wing (Light) was reactivated on 12 March 1951 with two squadrons, the 84th and 85th Bomb Squadrons, flying the B-45 Tornado. On 31 May 1952, the 47th Bombardment Wing was assigned to USAFE, being based at RAF Sculthorpe, Norfolk, England. During March of 1954, the Wing's third (and final) squadron, the 86th BS was formed. This squadron was destined not to remain at Sculthorpe for long and during September of 1955 it was moved to RAF Alconbury, Huntingdonshire.

The B-45s carried squadron markings consisting of a band painted across the top of the vertical fin in the appropriate squadron color: Red for the 84th, Yellow for the 85th and Blue for the 86th. This was later changed to a diagonal flash running across the fin with the last two numbers of the serial being repeated over the flash in large Black numbers.

A thin stripe was also painted horizontally on the aircraft's nose just below the bombardier's canopy (in the squadron color). This marking was eventually replaced with three stripes, one ahead of the 47th Wing badge and two following the badge, again in the squadron color.

25

This B-45A of the 85th Bomb Squadron, at the ramp at Shepherd's Grove, Suffolk, on 17th May 1958, has had the glass nose replaced by a solid nose. The aircraft also carries the legend, U.S. Air Force, in Black on the nose.

Another B-45 unit was the 19th TRS, which flew RB-45C Tornados. The unit was part of the 66th Tactical Reconnaissance Wing and was attached to the 47th Bomb Wing between May of 1954 and December of 1958. When the 19th TRS began to re-equip with RB-66s during 1957, its RB-45s were transferred to squadrons within the 47th Bomb Wing. The RB-45s carried the same markings as the B-45s, with the exception of a squadron marking on the wing tip fuel tanks. This marking consisted of two stripes coming back off the top and bottom of the circular squadron badge. The stripes were in the individual squadron color.

The Douglas B-66 Destroyer replaced the B-45s during 1958. The first sixteen aircraft were delivered on 18/19 January 1958, and assigned to the 84th Bomb Squadron. The 86th Squadron at RAF Alconbury followed, receiving its aircraft during May, while the 85th Squadron did not complete conversion until mid-July 1958.

After converting to the B-66, the three squadrons retained their individual colors and diagonal fin flash but deleted the nose markings. The 47th Wing badge was carried low on the port side of the nose just behind the radome with the squadron badge in the same position on the starboard side of the nose. During this time frame, the 86th Squadron returned to Sculthorpe from Alconbury joining the 84th and 85th Squadrons. The 86th carried an unusual marking in the form of a Black individual code letter on the rear fuselage just ahead of the tail guns.

The B-66 served with the 47th Bomb Wing until the unit was deactivated on 22 June 1962. A number of former 47th Wing aircraft were modified with the ECM tail and transferred to the 42TRS/10TRW at Chelveston Air Base during 1959.

During the time the 47th Wing served in USAFE, it operated a number of support aircraft such as C-119Gs, T-33As (two in each squadron), L-20s and a number of C-47As. The C-119s carried the same markings as the B-45s but in White with Black outlines, the C-47s were similar but carried squadron colors, while the T-33s and L-20s carried their respective squadron markings on the vertical stabilizer.

An RB-45C (of the 19th TRS) on the ramp at Sculthorpe, Norfolk, during 1954. The squadron was attached to the 47th Bomb Wing during 1954-1955. (D. Menard)

An RB-45C of the 84th Bomb Squadron, on the ramp at Wethersfield, Essex, of the base's 1957 Armed Forces Day Display. The Tornado carried the squadron badge on the wing tip fuel tanks. (Robinson collection)

A Douglas TB-26B Invader assigned to the 5th Target Tow Squadron (Detachment A), at Sculthorpe Air Base. The 5th TTS shared the base with the 47th Bomb Wing and the 420th Refueling Squadron during 1954. (G. Pennick)

5th TOW TARGET SQUADRON

Reactivated on 16 December 1952 as the 7554th Tow Target Flight at Furstenfeldbrück Air Base, Germany, the unit moved to Neubiberg, Germany, on 16 July 1954 and on 24 June 1954, it was redesignated the 5th Tow Target Squadron. For target towing duties, the squadron was equipped with TB-26B/C Invaders and a number of L-5 Sentinels.

The squadron markings consisted of Red and White horizontal stripes on the vertical and horizontal stabilizer and Red wing tips. Between 24 June 1954 and 15 May 1957, Detachment A (1) of the 5th Tow Target Squadron was stationed at RAF Sculthorpe, Norfolk. From here, the detachment flew target tow missions over the gunnery ranges around the Wash area with TB-26 aircraft.

This Douglas B-66B Destroyer was assigned to the 86th Bomb Squadron based at Sculthorpe Air Base, Norfolk, during 1961

A KB-50J tanker of the 420th Air Refueling Squadron. This was one of two aircraft known to have carried stripes around the wing tip refueling pods. The stripes were Blue, Yellow, Green and Red (front to rear) and the nosewheel door was Green with the aircraft serial in White. (MAP)

A Boeing SB-17G Flying Fortress of the Air Rescue Service during 1951-52. The fuselage and nose markings are in Yellow with a Black outline and the aircraft carried 83585 in Black under the port wing. (MAP)

420th AIR REFUELING SQUADRON

Formed as the 420th Air Refueling Squadron (Fighter-Bomber) on 8 December 1953 and activated on 18 March 1954, the squadron was based at Alexandria AFB, flying KB-29 tankers.

The squadron deployed to RAF Sculthorpe, Norfolk, England, on 4 October 1955 and was attached to the 47th Bombardment Wing to refuel F-84Fs and B/RB-45s. The KB-29s carried an overall metal finish with a Black triangle on the fin which contained a Blue, Yellow and Red design.

The KB-29s remained in operation until early 1959, being slowly replaced (from 1957 onward) by the faster KB-50. The KB-50s were used to refuel the Century series fighters and B-66s. Initially, the KB-50s were overall natural metal with Green nosewheel doors (which carried the aircraft's serial in White). During 1960, however, Red squadron markings were applied to the aircraft and these were carried until 1962, when they were deleted.

The 420th ARS remained in USAFE at RAF Sculthorpe until 25 March 1964, when it was officially deactivated.

AIR RESCUE SERVICE

Rescue duties within USAFE were the task of the 7th Air Rescue Squadron (ARS) based at Wheelus AFB, Libya (1945 to 1951) flying SB-17Gs, SC-47Ds and for a short time, SB-29s.

During late 1947, B-29s of the Strategic Air Command began arriving at USAF bases in Europe under the operational control of USAFE and the 3rd Air Division. During 1948, the 3rd Air Division moved to Bushy Park, sharing the facility with the 9th ARS (later enlarged to the 9th Rescue Group).

The Berlin crisis led to an increase in USAF deployments to Europe and, faced with this expansion, the Air Rescue Service was enlarged. The 9th Air Rescue Group (originally 9th ARS) was formed at Bushy Park during 1952, with three squadrons: the 66th ARS flying SA-16s and H-19A/Bs at RAF Manston, Kent (November 1952 to January 1958), 67th ARS with SA-16s, H-19s, SC-47s and SC-54Ds at Prestwick, Scotland (November 1953 to March 1960), and 68th ARS flying SB-17Gs from Burtenwood, Lancashire (1952 to 1958).

These units provided Air Rescue services within an area that extended from Iceland to West Germany and from Southern Europe to the North Pole. The 7th ARG covered the area from the Azores to Saudi Arabia, while the 12th ARG, with its headquarters at Ramstein, Germany, covered Central Europe. The 12th had squadrons operating from Sembach (81st ARS), Spangdalhem (82nd ARS), Furstenfeldbrück (83rd ARS) and Rhein Main (84th ARS).

Later, the 68th ARS at Burtonwood and the 66th ARS at Manston were absorbed by the 67th ARS at Prestwick during 1958. Two other units under USAFE were the 53rd ARS at Keflavick, Iceland and the 58th ARS at Wheelus, Libya. The latter unit operated SC-54s, SC-82s and SC-97s, along wih SA-16s and H-19s.

Rescue aircraft carried a Yellow, outlined in Black wide band around the rear fuselage, and had the aircraft's serial repeated below the wings in Yellow outlined in Black. They had a MATS badge on the rear fuselage and a Yellow band outlined in Black with the word Rescue in Black on the vertical fin. The 53rd ARS at Keflavick also carried Artic Red markings consisting of the entire tail section and the outer wing panels. High visibility Day-Glo Orange or Red markings were carried on SC-54s from 1959 to 1964 when most aircraft had the Day-Glo removed.

An HC-54D Searchmaster of the 67th Air Rescue Squadron, on the ramp at Preswick, Scotland, during 1960-61. The nose and tail markings are in Orange Day-Glo paint. The HC-54 had large observation windows installed in the fuselage alongside the rear door. (MAP)

A KB-50J on final approach for landing. The aircraft was assigned to the 420th Air Refueling Squadron during 1961 and carried Red squadron markings on the fin, wing tip refueling pods and jet engine pods. (MAP)

A WB-50D assigned to the 53rd Weather Reconnaissance Squadron during the Armed Forces Day Display at Alconbury Air Base, Huntingdonshire, on 16 May 1959 (MAP)

A natural metal Martin RB-57A of the 30th Tactical Reconnaissance Squadron, 66th Tactical Reconnaissance Wing displayed on the ramp at Wethersfield for Armed Forces Day (16 May 1957). (G. Pennick)

53rd WEATHER RECONNAISSANCE SQUADRON

The 53rd Weather Reconnaissance Squadron was reactivated on 21 February 1951 with three flights stationed at Kindley Field, Bermuda. The division of the squadron into flights and the deployment of these flights to various locations was required by the nature of the unit's mission and responsibilities. The 53rd WRS was responsible for weather reconnaissance over large geographical areas, most of which was over water. Its aircraft collected data both for Air Force weather forecasts and for the U.S. Weather Bureau.

From 1951 until 1953 the 53rd WRS flew WB-29s along tracks ranging out of Bermuda. On 7 November 1953, the squadron moved to RAF Burton Wood, Lancashire, England, under the control of the 9th Weather Group (although one flight remained on Bermuda). Most reconnaissance missions from England were along triangular tracks to the Northeast and Northwest, out to 70 degrees North latitude.

After 25 November, the 9th Weather Group was redesignated as the 2058th Air Weather Wing. The routes flown by the wing were known as Falcon Tracks and Atlantic flights were known as Falcon Golf Tracks. During 1956, the WB-50 replaced the WB-29 and the wing designation was changed to the 2nd Weather Wing.

Later, the Falcon Golf Track was lengthened and renamed Falcon Delta. Falcon Delta missions departed RAF Burtonwood at 0700 daily. The track was 3,686 miles long and extended from Liverpool to a point 250 miles North of the Azores, then turned North along the 30th Meridian to a point 420 miles Southeast of Greenland and finally turned East towards Burtonwood. The first leg of the mission was flown at 10,000 feet, with the second being flown at 18,000 feet and the final leg at 30,000 feet. The mission had an average flight time of some fifteen hours, with weather observations being made at fixed points 150nm apart.

The weatherman was seated in the nose of the aircraft and recorded the wind speed and direction, pressure, himidity, temperature, cloud conditions, visibility, surface winds and pack ice conditions (if present). Radar findings were added to the report before it was coded by the radio operator and sent to Croughton Radio Station. From here it was retransmitted to the 53rd Weather Monitor at Burtonwood, where it was decoded and checked for transmission errors before being teletyped to the Central Weather Station at High Wycombe.

On 2 April 1956 Falcon Golf was replaced by a daily flight known as Falcon Echo which, while still an Atlantic track, went much farther south. The Falcon Echo track ran South to the Madeira Islands, then Northward to a point on the 26 degree West Meridian near the Azores, then almost due North East back to England. The last Falcon Echo mission out of Burtonwood took place on 22 April 1959 and, when the WB-50 completed its mission, it landed at RAF Alconbury, the new home base for the 53rd WRS.

The WB-50s had all armament deleted and an air sampling pod mounted on top of the rear fuselage. Internally, the bomb bay housed a jettisonable bladder fuel tank capable of holding 10,000 gallons of fuel. The aircraft were overall Aluminum with the vertical stabilizer,

horizontal stabilizers and outer wing panels in Red. The MATS badge was carried on the rear fuselage sides and a Dark Blue band, bordered in Yellow with the legend, Weather, superimposed on the band in White. Later, WB-50s had the upper half of the fuselage painted White.

The 53rd Weather Reconnaissance Squadron was transferred to RAF Mildenhall on 10 August 1959, and flights out of England were discontinued on 18 March 1960.

66th TACTICAL RECONNAISSANCE WING

The 66th Tactical Reconnaissance Group (TRG) was reactivated on 1 January 1953 and equipped with RB-26 and RF-80 aircraft. The Group was assigned to USAFE during June/July of 1953 and based at Sembach, Germany.

The 66th TRG had four squadrons: the 302nd TRS flying RF-80s (squadron color, Red), 303rd TRS with RF-80s (Blue), 19th TRS equipped with RB-45s (Blue) and the 30th TRS with RB-26s (Yellow). Three squadrons, the 302nd, 303rd and 30th were based at Sembach, Germany, while the 19th TRS was attached to the 47th Bombardment Wing at RAF Sculthorpe, Norfolk, England.

Early markings carried by the Sembach based squadrons consisted of a double chevron on the vertical stabilizer with the point of the chevron at the front of the fin. The chevron was sometimes also carried on the wing tip tanks of the RF-80s and RB-57As. The RF-80s and RB-57s carried the chevron painted in the appropriate squadron color. The RB-45s of the 19th TRS at RAF Sculthorpe, Norfolk, carried a Dark Blue band across the vertical stabilizer with three White stars. The wing tip tanks also had a Dark Blue band on the outer portion of the tank again with three White stars. A Blue stripe was painted on the aircraft's nose running back to the rear of the crew entry door.

Usually, the 66th Wing badge was carried on the starboard forward fuselage with the squadron badge on the port side. The 19th TRS, however, carried the squadron badge on both sides of the fuselage (it is believed unlikely that badges were carried on the RF-80s and RB-26s). During 1954, both the 302nd TRS and 303rd TRS were

This RB-66B Destroyer carries the markings of the 19th TRS. The 19th was assigned to the 66th Tactical Reconnaissance Wing, at Wiesbaden, Germany, during 1957. (G. Joos)

re-equipped with RF-84Fs, while the 30th TRS re-equipped with RB-57As during 1955.

During 1957, the Sembach based squadrons changed their markings. The chevrons were replaced by a tail band which tapered from front to rear. The band was in the appropriate squadron color with four White stars superimposed on it. A similar design was painted on the outer portion of the wing tip tanks and drop tanks.

In February of 1957, the 19th TRS began to re-equip with RB-66s and by May of that year the squadron was nearly at full strength. The RB-66s carried a Dark Blue band with White stars around the engine nacelle and Wing/Squadron badges were carried in the normal positions.

During January of 1958, the 66th Wing was reorganized. Upon completion of the reorganization, the 66th Wing was equipped with RF-84Fs. Its RB-66 units were transferred to the 10th TRW (while the 10th's RF-84F units went to the 66th TRW). The wing now consisted of the 32nd TRS, 38th TRS at Phalsbourg Air Base, France, and the 302nd and 303rd TRS. Squadron color assignments were as follows: Red (302 TRS), Blue (303rd TRS), Yellow (32nd TRS) and Green (38th TRS). The White star markings were retained, although wing and squadron badges were rarely carried.

By 1959, the Wing had re-equipped with the RF-101C and the 302nd and 303rd squadrons had been replaced by the 17th TRS and 18th TRS, respectively.

Support Aircraft

Operational units also operated a number of aircraft in the support role, usually known as hacks. These aircraft were used for transporting personnel and cargo between bases, proficiency training, and for checking out new personnel. A squadron usually had one or more T-33s, at least one C-47 and sometimes an L-20. Each base had a Base Flight which was responsible for maintenance and ground support for these aircraft.

These aircraft, although somewhat overshadowed by the front line aircraft, were often more colorful and, in a number of cases, carried a different style of markings than the normal aircraft within the squadron.

During 1955/56, the T-33s of the 10th TRW originally carried the same arrow design as the unit's RB-57s and RF-84s. Later, during 1957/58 when new markings were introduced on the RB-66s, the unit applied a similar design to their C-47s. These markings consisted of a Black shooting star with three Red tails carried on either side of the tail and the 10th Wing badge placed behind the cockpit superimposed over the silhouette of a Red camera. The unit's T-33s carried the same style of markings, with the addition of a diagonal stripe across the tail in the appropriate squadron color. T-33s painted in Overall Gloss Light Gray carried the same tail markings without the diagonal band.

These markings were carried until 1961. The C-47s deleted all colorful insignia but the T-33s retained the colorful markings until 1962 when a new marking system was adopted, comprised of a Black shooting star with a four-colored plume coming off the star. This marking was carried on the vertical stabilizer of the T-33s.

During 1959/60, a high visibility Red/Orange paint was introduced for support aircraft. Normally, Red/Orange panels were carried on

This Douglas C-47A Skytrain was flown by the 66th Tactical Reconnaissance Group Headquarters Flight, based at Sembach, Germany, during 1956. (D. W. Menard)

the nose, in a band around the rear fuselage and on the outer wing panels (and tip tanks). Despite the use of the high visibility markings, squadron and wing markings were retained (although usually removed from the T-33 wing tip tanks). The 20th TFW applied their lightning streak design to the fuselage, tail and wing tip tanks on their T-33s during 1958, in appropriate squadron colors. During 1959/1960, the individual squadron colors were replaced by a three colored streak on the tail and wing tanks. Their C-47s also carried this three colored streak along the fuselage top, while the wings of the L-20s and T-39s carried similar markings.

The 36th Fighter Group carried Blue and White stripes on the tail surfaces of their C-47s and on the nose and tail of their T-33s, with a Red diagonal band on the wings. During 1955, this was changed to three diagonal bands being carried across the aircraft's tail in the appropriate squadron color. By 1961 these bands were changed to three colors, representing the markings of the wing.

The 47th Bomb Wing adopted the same style of markings for their C-47s and C-119s as was used on the unit's B-45s except that they were in White with Black trim lines. T-33s and L-20s also carried similar markings, with the tail markings in the squadron color. By 1962, the majority of the markings had been replaced by high visibility Red/Orange panels.

One T-33 of the 48th TFW was noted carrying a design originating from the *Statue de la Liberte* Wing badge on the tail. These were trial markings and had been used on a number of the Wing's F-86Fs during 1954 and 1955.

Aircraft of the 50th TFW carried markings consisting of three colored tail bands of Red, Yellow and Blue with White and Black stars (C-47s) and the 50th Wing emblem superimposed on the center band. These aircraft also carried high visibility Red/Orange markings. Later, the high visibility markings were deleted, and the aircraft were repainted in an overall Gloss Light Gray with the upper half of the fuselage in White. These aircraft retained the tail colors, although in reverse order.

The 50th TFW L-20s also carried the same style markings but in reverse order on the tail. Until 1960 these markings were also carried on the engine cowling in the form of a chevron. These were later removed when the cowlings were repainted in high visibility Red/Orange. 50th TFW T-33s carried the same markings as their C-47s.

The 66th TRW aircraft during 1955/56 all carried the basic Wing markings of two chevrons (in the squadron color) on the aircraft's vertical stabilizer. One C-47 was noted carrying a long lightning streak along the upper fuselage and a chevron on the tail in Red, Yellow, Blue and Green with the 66th Wing badge carried behind the cockpit. Later, 66th TRW T-33s and L-20s carried a broad diagonal

An H-19 of the 10th TRW Base Flight at Toul-Rosieres Air Base, France, during June of 1959. The aircraft in the background is an RAF Supermarine Swift reconnaissance fighter. (D. W. Menard)

This C-47D Skytrain carries the markings of the 21st Fighter-Bomber Wing Base Flight at Chambley, France, during 1955-56. (A. Pearcy)

An L-20A of the 21st Fighter-Bomber Wing Base Flight at Wiesbaden, Germany, during 1955-56. The L-20 was used as a station hack to ferry men and supplies from one base to another. (G. Joos)

This AT-6 Texan (44-81737), assigned to the 36th Fighter Group Headquarters Flight, carried Medium Blue and White stripes around both the vertical and horizontal tail surfaces during 1954. (L. Kelly)

A Douglas C-47D Skytrain transport assigned to the 405th Bomb Squadron, 38th Bomb Wing at Laon Air Base, France, during 1955-56. (A Pearcy)

White/Black/White band across the tail. By 1962, this had given way to a sunburst marking consisting of four colors radiating from a Yellow star on a Dark Blue circle.

During 1956/57, the T-33s of the 81st FBW carried a White Atomic cloud design on a Blue crest with the 81st Wing badge superimposed on the cloud. The nose, fuselage and tail carried Blue, Yellow, and Red stripes. One L-20 carried a Blue, Yellow and Red fuselage flash with a White atomic cloud and Wing badge, Blue, Yellow and Red wing tips and a Red checkerboard engine cowling.

By 1960, these markings had been replaced on the T-33s and L-20s by the late style 81st Wing badge, carried on the tail, and high visibility Red/Orange areas on the fuselage and wings. The L-20 had the Red checkerboard cowling replaced by an overall Red cowling. The C-47s carried a standard scheme of overall natural metal with White uppersurfaces and Red/Orange areas. They normally carried the Wing badge behind the cockpit. The T-33s and L-20s later adopted the same style markings as carried on the Wing's F-101s.

86th FIW C-47s carried a Blue and Yellow sunburst design on the aircraft's tail during 1959/1960.

Another unit that used colorful markings on their T-33s was the 514th FIS, 406th FIW. The T-33s carried three colored tail bands superimposed with the 514th FIS badge. Additionally, the cockpit sill and wing tip tanks were painted Blue.

The T-33s of the 431st FIS carried the unit's Satan's Head insignia on a red band on the vertical stabilizer. The unit was based at Zaragosa Air Base, Spain, during 1960.

A Lockheed T-33A Shooting Star assigned to the 77th Fighter-Bomber Squadron, 20th Fighter-Bomber Group at Wethersfield on display for the base's 1954 Armed Forces Day Open House (15 May 1954). (G Pennick)

This C-47A Skytrain, assigned to the 36th Fighter Group Headquarters Flight at Blackbushe on 8 September 1955, also carried the 36th FG's Medium Blue and White tail stripes. (R. A. Scholefield)

(Above) A Fairchild C-119F Flying Boxcar assigned to the 47th Bomb Wing Base Flight, on the ramp at Greenham Common during May of 1956. (MAP)

(Below) This T-33A Shooting Star of the 50th Tactical Fighter Wing at Toul Rosiers Air Base, France, carried a large Buzz number in Black on the fuselage side. (D. W. Menard)

(Below) This C-47A was assigned to the 50th Tactical Fighter Wing Headquarters Flight at Toul Rosiers Air Base, France, during June of 1959. The aircraft carries an unusually long serial number on the fin. (D. W. Menard)

(Above) Flown by the 20th Fighter-Bomber Group Headquarters Flight during 1959, this T-33A carried three color markings like those carried on the aircraft of their parent Wing. (MAP)

(Below) A C-47A of the 86th Fighter-Bomber Wing Headquarters Flight at Blackbushe Air Base during 1956-57. (MAP)

An armed T-33A Shooting Star of the 19th TRS is being refueled on the ramp of its English home base. The squadron was attached to the 47th Bomb Wing during 1955-56. (D. W. Menard)

This L-20A, assigned to the 78th Fighter-Bomber Squadron, 81st Fighter-Bomber Wing at Woolbrige, Suffolk, on 18 May 1957, carried a Red checkered cowling. (A. Wright)